Any Fool Can Do Magic!

A Jester's Guide to Becoming a Great Magician

Including Instructions for
Nearly 100 Easy To Do Magic Tricks

By
Jon Koons
(JestMaster Wince the WowBeGone)

Illustrated by Irv Koons
Foreword by Marvin Kaye

This is an original publication of Metamorphic Press

Cover Art by StrikingImages.com

ISBN: 978-1-951221-17-1

First published by Ye Olde Cambridge Jester's Academy - 1995
First Metamorphic Edition printing March 2021

Published by:
Metamorphic Press
PO 151 Box
Tenafly, NJ 07670
metamorphicpress.com

Proudly Printed in the United States of America

So you want to be a Great Magician?

Here's How...

Ye Olde Foreword

Any fool can do magic... and usually does! In America alone, some twenty thousand amateurs, young and old, spend lots of money buying magic tricks, but few learn how to do them well. Instead, they bore their families and friends (if they've got any left after they do their first few bad shows).

This book contains almost one hundred fun magic tricks that are simple to learn and perform, but even the easiest take time to master. In your eagerness to show these wonders, don't neglect to read and heed the showmanship tips in the opening pages . . . especially this one:

Practice, Practice, Practice!

How long do you have to practice before appearing before an audience? A lot longer than you think. The easiest trick needs to be rehearsed over and over again. Becoming a real entertainer always takes time.

Here's how to know if you're ready to show a trick to people:

H ave you learned the hand movements so well that you don't have to think about them? If you can't practically do them in your sleep, you haven't practiced them enough.

M any tricks have a "danger spot" when the secret might be noticed. Do you know where it is? Do you know how to minimize the risk? Good magicians plan ways to cover up these places. If, for instance, your right hand must make a move that nobody is supposed to see, you might distract the audience with some movement of your left hand at that time in the trick. Or you might tell a joke. Or ask the audience a question that makes them raise their hands. There are many ways to cover up "danger spots" and they must be practiced as much as the basic hand movements.

D o you know what you're going to say while you perform a trick? Whatever it is, this "patter" has to be rehearsed, too. But be careful! In your first public magic shows, don't be surprised if members of your audience say things that are not in the script you made up in your head. If they do, just smile and answer them cleverly, if you can. If not, smile and ignore them . . . but be polite and pleasant about it. After all, you are supposed to be entertaining them. If they actually guess how a trick is done, you can always smile and say, "You might be right, but then again, you might not. And a good magician never tells his secrets." Then do another trick that totally fools them!

Above all, remember that you can't really make solid objects pass through other objects, appear out of nowhere, disappear or defy gravity. If you could do those things, you wouldn't need this book. You're an actor playing the part of a magician. Good actors learn how to move well and speak well and interact pleasantly with their audiences. A good magician practices these same skills.

So if you're not just any fool, you'll heed the advice in this book and become the best magician you can be.

Marvin Kaye
Author of *The Handbook of Magic*
The Handbook of Mental Magic
Catalog of Magic
and a whole bunch of other stuff

Ye Olde Introduction

I n the days of kings and castles, the Court
Jesters, who were also called fools, buffoons,
merrymakers and such, were very important
people. It was their job to amuse the kings,
queens, popes and guests of the royal court. If
one was powerful and wealthy enough he would
have a fool, or several, to keep him entertained
whenever the whim struck him. Many Jesters
were so well respected that they became trusted
advisors and companions to their masters and
mistresses. Jesters, who came in all shapes and
sizes, both male and female, were the earliest
versions of what today are called comedians and
clowns.

A Jester's main job was to make people
laugh. They did this in a number of ways,
from telling jokes and making up rhymes
to putting on acts and plays to simply
falling down and acting silly. But Jesters also
used many other methods to entertain.
Although the Minstrel was the official singer
and musician, and Bards the story tellers of the
period, Jesters were always ready with a funny

song and a quick-witted story. It was common for Jesters to play a variety of instruments. While poets would write beautiful verse, many Jesters were just as skilled with language and used their own poems to captivate their audiences. Plays were written and performed by playwrights and actors, but Jesters did that too. Indeed, many Jesters were also poets, singers, writers and actors in addition to their jobs as Court Jester. Jesters were so well loved and respected, that many even held jobs such as lawyers, statesman and university professors when they were not at work amusing the kings.

Magic is something that Jesters also used to entertain. While the Court Wizard or local Magician would be responsible for the "real" magic needed by the people (there was a time when magic was considered very real, and wizards used to help kings rule, help doctors heal, and help explain the mysteries of the world) the Jester did simple tricks that would make the audience applaud at the outcome and wonder at how they were done, but not make them fearful of natural (real) or black (evil) magic.

The Magician's Art

Magic is one of the world's oldest and most respected arts, going back thousands of years, and it is logical to assume that Jesters, always looking for ways to entertain, included it among the many skills they displayed. Today, although magicians rarely help rule, heal, or explain the world's mysteies, they are just as important in the same way that Jesters once were. Magicians entertain people, make them laugh, amaze them, and make them forget their problems for a little while.

These days, the dictionary defines magic as:
1- The Art of Producing Illusions.
2- Having Seemingly Supernatural Powers.
3- Giving a Feeling of Enchantment.

One who can do all of these things is called **MAGICIAN**.

But there are other words that also mean the same thing. So if you are a MAGICIAN, you are also a:

Prestidigitator
Conjurer
Sorcerer
Wizard
Magi
Mystic
Legerdemainist
Genie
Illusionist

And a bunch of other names. Can you find out what they are?

Since the beginning of the magical arts, practiced by real Wizards or just Jesters, there were and still are only seven basic magic effects (tricks). All magic tricks are different versions of these seven. They are:

1. Appearance

Making something out of nothing.

2. Disappearance

Making something into nothing.

3. Levitation

Making something rise into the air.

4. Suspension

Making something float in one place.

5. Transformation

Making something change into something else.

6. Transportation

Making something move someplace else.

7. Penetration

Making something solid pass through something else.

As a magician, you will learn to do all these things. As a Jester, you can present all of the magic that you learn in especially fun and entertaining ways. Once you have learned the simple rules that follow and the basic magic tricks in this book, you too can amaze and entertain, and take your place among those who have made magic the most popular form of entertainment in the world.

And now it's time to learn how to Amuse and Amaze!

The Most Important Rule Of Magic Is Secrecy. A Magician May Never Tell His Secrets To Anyone Except Another Magician. This Is Why.

The Secret's The Thing

W hat makes magic seem magical? Magic is magic because people don't know how things happen. If you make one card rise up out of a deck of cards, you know how to do it, BUT THE AUDIENCE DOESN'T! If they did, it wouldn't be magic. That's why it is so important not to tell your secrets.

I f you tell the secret, the audience knows how the trick is done, it no longer seems like magic, and you can't repeat the same trick again. So, if you tell a secret you're ruining your own performances, and those of other magicians. Some magicians never even tell their secrets to other magicians! So, to become a good magician, you must remember:

Never reveal your secrets!

To Be Good At Anything, Not Only Magic,
Requires Practice. But Practice Is
Especially Important For Magicians.
This Is Why.

Practice Makes Perfect

If you want to play the piano for some friends and make a mistake, all you have to do is start over again and play it right. But in magic, if you make a mistake, you give away the secret. If the audience knows how it's done, there is no more mystery to the trick, and you can't do it over again.

To do any trick, you must practice it until you can do it perfectly. The better you perform the trick, the more magical it will appear. The more practice you have, the better you will perform the trick, amaze your audience and seem professional.

After you have learned how to do a trick, practice it in front of a mirror. This way you will be able to see what the audience sees. Sometimes even if it looks right to you, the audience can see something you don't want them to see. After you've practiced in front of a mirror until you think you're just about perfect, you can show the trick to another magician so that he can point out any problems he may see. If there are no other magicians around, appoint one friend (but only one) who you can practice all your tricks with. He can tell you if the trick looks magical enough— but you have to make him promise not to tell anyone else how it is done! Remember, to become a first rate magician, you must

Practice, Practice, Practice!

To Perform Magic And Entertain An Audience,
Showmanship Is Very Important.
This Is Why.

Showmanship Makes The Difference

W ith enough practice almost anyone can learn to do a trick. But to really be a magician, that trick has to be presented in a way that makes it magic. Magicians are showmen. Doing magic should entertain people, make them laugh and have an enjoyable time. If you can amaze them too, that's even better.

B ut how can you entertain and amaze them? Remember what we said about Jesters. All of the different ways that they entertain people and make them laugh: telling jokes, making up rhymes, putting on acts, singing songs and telling stories. You can use all of these methods to make your trick entertaining as well as magical. To get you started, here are two main ways to present an entertaining and amazing magic trick. They are **Entertain with Patter** and **Amaze with Misdirection.**

Entertain With Patter

Patter is a word used in magic to describe the stories and jokes that you tell while you do a trick. Patter is very important. It can turn an ordinary trick into a wonderfully interesting and entertaining one.

Here is an example. Let's say you are going to make a matchbox move. You could say:
"Watch the box... it's going to move."

You *could* say that, but that is very boring, and people might think "So who cares if it moves?"

Or you could say:
"This is a very special matchbox. It is haunted. Now if you look very closely, you might be able to see the spirits inside it. Look, the spirits are moving the box!"

Now, it's more entertaining. It's not just a trick that you did, but might even involve spirits and real magic!

Or you could tell a joke to go along with the trick. For example, if you are doing the floating egg trick you could present it like this:

"You've seen those commercials on TV for tuna fish called 'Chicken of the Sea.' Well, I've got the real chicken of the sea at home. No really, I do. I'll prove it to you. She laid this special egg. It's an egg of the sea and it likes to swim. I see you don't believe me. Well, just watch! When I put it into salty sea water it floats. Isn't that egg-citing?

Always make up a good story or tell some good jokes when you do a trick. This will make it much more fun, and people will want you to do more.

Amaze With Misdirection

Misdirection is getting people to look where you want them to. This is how you can do many things without the audience seeing you do them. There are a number of ways in which you can misdirect a person. The best and easiest way is to look at them while you are talking to them. If you are looking into a person's eyes while you are talking, he will want to look back. This way he's not looking at your hands.

Another way is by looking at something else or by motioning somewhere else. For example, if you pretend to put something in your hand, hold that hand up in the air and look at it. Everyone else will look too. While they are looking there (and listening to your entertaining patter) you can hide the object that is really in your other hand.

By using misdirection properly, your tricks will seem much more magical and you will be a better magician.

When You Do Magic You Should Not Do The
Same Trick Over Again For The Same People.
This Is Why.

The Hands Are
Slower Than
The Eye

There's an old saying in magic . . . "The
hand is quicker than the eye." Well,
although it sounds catchy, it's just not
true. The eyes can see things much faster
than the hands can move. The only reason
people can't see what you don't want them to is
because of misdirection.

When you show a trick to someone, he
often will ask you to do it again. That is
something you should never do.

Because he saw the trick once, he knows
what's going to happen, so he is going to be
looking much more carefully at what you
are doing. When he does this, he might just
catch a mistake, or figure out how the trick is

done (and you know how important it is to keep your secrets!). So don't do the same trick for the same people, at least not right away. You can do it again after a couple of days, but not earlier

I f you don't repeat the same tricks for the same people, you can keep your secrets safe and become a fine magician!

*If You Want To Do Magic For Many People,
It Is Important That They Know Who
You Are. This Is Why.*

What Is A Good Magical Name?

I f people like the way you do magic, they will tell others about you. When they do, the easier it is to remember your name, the better.

A lthough many magicians use their own names, many add to them to make them sound more magical. One of the easiest ways to do this is by alliteration. Alliteration means using a word with the same first letter or letter sounds as yours. You can use your first or last name. For example:

Miller The Magician
The Amazing Andy
Mystical Melanie
Kelly The Colossal

nother way is to change your own name to sound more magical. In Vaudeville days magicians used to honor their magical heroes by making their own names sound similar. Harry Houdini, one of the greats, is the best example. For example: The name Ogden becomes **OGDINI** like "Houdini." The name Danny becomes **HOUDANNY**, also like "Houdini."

ou can also make up a new name completely. For example: **Mysto** or the **Magical Man.** Of course, if you are going to do magic as a Jester, you should use a comical name that suits your character, like **Winkle** or **Boffo** or even **Twinkie.**

hen you find a stage name you like, stick with it. If you keep changing your stage name, people will get confused. Once your name becomes known, you will be asked to perform all the time!

What Does A Magician Look Like?

M agicians can be all kinds of people. Guys, girls, tall, short, fat, skinny, young, old . . . just like Jesters! But all of these people have something in common. When they are performing magic, they are all dressed appropriately for the character they become.

M agicians wear different things, depending on the type of act they want. If you are going to perform as a Jester, you need to be very colorful with bells and a funny hat. If you want to do magic dressed as a clown, you need the right costume and make-up. Some magicians wear a top hat and a cape. Others wear a suit, or special colorful costumes. But there is only one rule as to how a magician should dress. He or she should be neat and clean looking.

If you are wearing ripped jeans and a t-shirt, who is going to want to watch you? Make sure you dress neatly, and that your hair is combed and your face washed. You also have to make especially sure that your hands and fingernails are clean. They are what people are going to be looking at most. As long as you are neat and clean, people will respect you and want to watch you.

If, as you start performing for more and more people, you want to have a special costume for magic, decide what kind would be best for your act. Do you want to look formal? Do you want to look casual? Or colorful, or scary, or mystical? Do you want to be a specific character when you do magic, like a Jester, a clown, a wizard, or an exotic Swami or even an alien? (If you want to be a character that's a great tradition, but if you are then it's not just all about the costume— you need the right voice and accent and story to edxplain who you are and all that stuff too!) When you decide what is best for you, you can create a costume that will impress everyone, and prove to them that you are a great magician as soon as they see you step before them.

Here are some looks that I use doing different kinds of magic shows for different occasions:

*If You've Learned All The Rules Of Magic
That You Just Read And Are Going To
Follow Them, You Are Ready To Become
A Great Magician.*

Now You're Ready!

L earn several of the tricks that follow, a few from each section. Pick your favorites, and organize them into a show, alternating between magic types. It is more interesting and exciting to have an appearance followed by a penetration, followed by a transportation, etc., then having several of the same type trick all in a row. Also mix the order of tricks using different props, so you do a money trick, a food trick, a card trick and so on instead of repeating the same types. Scatter in some of the "joke" tricks, just for fun. Now practice, practice practice! Keep it up until you are perfect, and don't have to think about how to do a trick but can just let it happen automatically. Come up with appropriate patter, jokes and stories for each trick— then practice some more.

It sounds like a lot of work, but it's worth it. When you rehearse that much you'll know everything so well that you probably won't even be nervous! (Don't worry if you are. Even magicians and Jesters who have been doing it for years still get a little nervous.) When you finally perform your show for people, with the tricks in the order you've set up, the patter you've rehearsed and the costume you've selected, you will be a big hit. (Or you may not be the first few times. But you'll learn and improve until you are!) Make sure to stop between each trick for applause, and be sure to bow and thank your audience at the end of the show!

Always have a trick with you, so that when people ask you to, you can do a trick upon request.

So...

How are you doing?
How's your patter?
Your misdirection?
Have you practiced enough?
Do you look neat and clean?
Do you have a magical name?
Are you keeping your secrets?

If you can answer all these questions with confidence, then you are on your way to becoming a great magician.

You Are Now Ready To Perform Friends, Family And Other Audiences.

Use the last several pages of this book to work out your show– write down your own performing ideas, patter, show order, costume ideas and all that stuff!

Good Luck!

Or as we say in show biz . . .

Break a Leg!

(Don't ask me why.)

Ye Olde Magical Effects

Fantastical Food

Implements of Writing

Money Miraculous

Crafty Cards

Mystic Matches

Items Common

FANTASTICAL FOOD

Magic with food is always popular because everybody has got to eat!
Sometimes, when a magician uses a special prop, like a magic box or tube, people think "it's not really magic because it must be a trick box," but magic with food is something everyone can identify with. If you take out a banana or cookie or egg, people will always know it is real (even if it isn't!)

Magic with food is also popular because it makes the magic more "real" for people. If you can do magic with something that people see every day at the dinner table, then you must be a fine magician indeed!
Another benefit is that after some food tricks you can eat the evidence, again proving that the food is real and so is the magic!

A Magic Snack
Wave your magic wand and then realize that you haven't eaten yet. Magicians have to eat magical food, so you eat your wand!

The secret is to make a wand out of a stick of black licorice. Wet the tips and dip into white sugar. A real looking wand, and a tasty snack!

YUMMY!

Roping An Ice Cube
Challenge a friend to take an ice cube out of a glass of water using a piece of string. He can't but you can!

The secret is to rest a coil or two of strong on top of the ice cube. Now sprinkle some salt on the ice and string. Wait a few moments. The salt melts the ice, then it refreezes around the string. You can now lift the ice cube with the string!

Can Exchange

Hold up a can of beets and a can of peas. Put beets in a paper bag, put peas in another bag. Take each can out to show the labels again. Cans have changed places.

The secret is that before starting, carefully cut a duplicate set of labels. Wrap cans with opposite labels . . . tape edges. Fold tape back to make a tiny flap. Flip of false label when returning can to bag.

Salt 'N' Pepper

Pour a small pile of salt on the table. Now drop a few grains of pepper into the salt. Say that you are going to separate the salt and pepper in only a couple of seconds. Nobody thinks you can, but you do!

The secret is to use a hair comb. Run it through your hair a few times, or on your shirt (if it's made of wool). The static electricity created will make the pepper cling to the comb when you run it through the pile of salt.

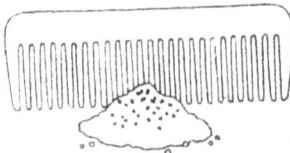

Gum's Gone

Put a piece of gum in one hand and hide both
hands behind your back. Bring forward. Ask
which hand it's in. They pick wrong. Repeat a
few times. Finally open both hands. It's gone!

The secret is to hide the gum in your back
pocket when your hands are behind your back.

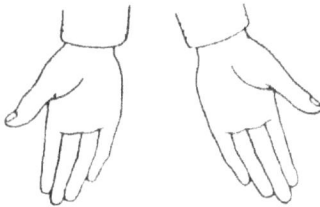

Attracting Sugar

Challenge a friend to make a toothpick come to
an ordinary sugar cube. He can't, but you can!

The secret is to let the toothpick float in a bowl
of water. Tie a threat around the sugar cube, and
lower it about half way into the water about an
inch from the toothpick. Toothpick will come to
the sugar cube.

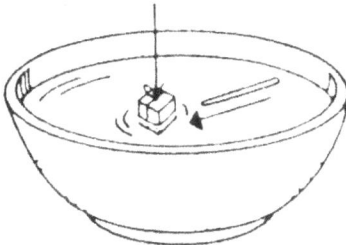

Dizzy Bug

You have several eggs and plates. Take an egg and a plate, and have your friends each do the same. Now tell them to spin the egg. No one does it but you!

The secret is to use a hard boiled egg. A hard boiled egg will spin, but an uncooked egg won't.

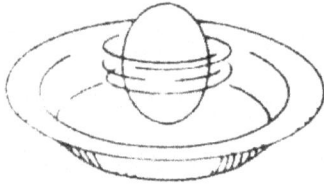

Light Egg

Hand a friend a glass of water and keep one yourself. Now hand him an egg and tell him to make it float. He can't. Use the same egg in your glass and it floats!

The secret is to fill your glass about a third full of salt before adding water. Stir until clear. Egg will float in saltwater.

Candy Sparks

This is a strange trick. Turn off the lights, and when it is dark people looking in your direction will hear crunching noises and see faint blue sparks!

The secret is wintergreen flavored Lifesavers. As you bite one, it makes faint blue sparks that can be seen in the dark. Be careful when you bite them, they're hard!

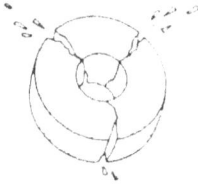

Bonkers Banana

Ask your friends to call out numbers from 1 to 10 and write them down on pieces of paper and put into a hat. Have someone pick one. It says "3". Pick up a banana, peel it, and it is cut into three pieces.

The secret is to write number 3 on each paper. They have to pick 3. To cut the banana, use a pin. Stick it in two places and move from side to side. This cuts banana into 3 without cutting the skin.

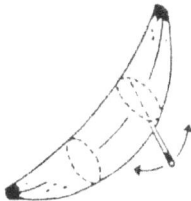

Tasty Candle

You have a candle on the table for decoration. You realize that you are hungry, and you eat the candle, wick and all!

The secret is to cut a banana into the shape of a candle. Use a bit of almond or brazil nut for the wick. It will really burn. If you only need a small candle, use an apple instead of a banana. It's a little easier since it's harder.

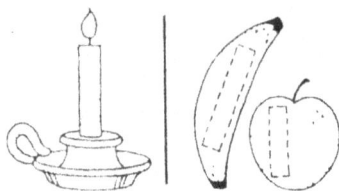

A Sticky Situation

Cover your thumb with a hanky, and stick pins into it without hurting yourself.

The secret is to hide a piece of carrot in your hand and put it under the hanky where your thumb should be sticking up! Push pins in. When you take the pins out, remove the carrot with the hanky, and show your thumb unharmed.

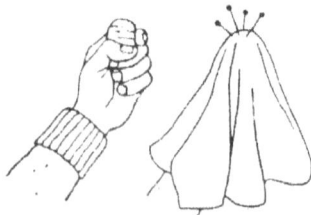

Upright Egg

Challenge a friend to balance an egg on its end. He can't, but you can!

The secret is to put some salt under the tablecloth. Put the egg in the middle of the salt, large end down, and it will balance.

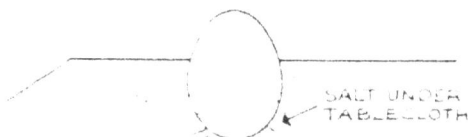

SALT UNDER TABLECLOTH

Magical Lollipops

Take four different colored lollipops from a bag, one at a time, and put each back. Take out your favorite one. Give bag to a friend to take one. They've all vanished!

The secret is to make one double-headed lollipop with each face painted a different color. Wrap in cellophane. Show different side each time by turning the stick in bag.

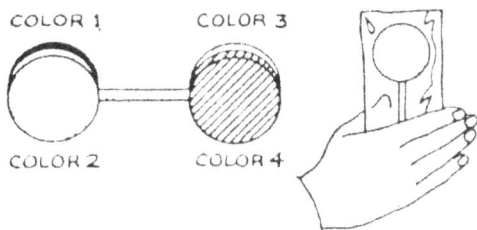

COLOR 1   COLOR 3

COLOR 2   COLOR 4

IMPLEMENTS OF WRITING

Since the dawn of civilization, when the first pictures were being drawn and (more than a few years later) the first words were written, magicians have used the implements of writing as magical props.

Of course, back then they wrote with a stylus (stick) on a wax covered slate, or used bird's feathers as pens, and roughly crafted homemade papers. Today a magician has a much more varied assortment of writing implements to choose from. Pencils, ball point pens, markers and more. And papers are nice and square and smooth and come in all colors.

These common items are always popular for doing magic because they are always close at hand and easily available. And magic using familiar items is always more impressive.

Rubber Pencil

Borrow a pencil or pen, showing that it is
ordinary. Say the magic words, wave it in the
air, and it looks like it is made out of rubber.

The secret is to hold the pencil with your thumb
and first finger loosely, and wave your hand up
and down, using short moves. The pencil looks
bendy. It takes practice, but it's worth it.

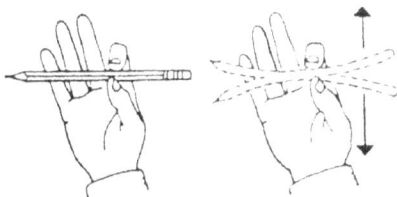

Strong Paper

Put 2 paper cups about 5 inches apart, and place
a piece of paper on top of them. Challenge your
friends to make another cup stand on top of the
top of the paper in the center without falling
through. They can't but you can!

The secret is to fold the paper like an accordion,
as in the picture.

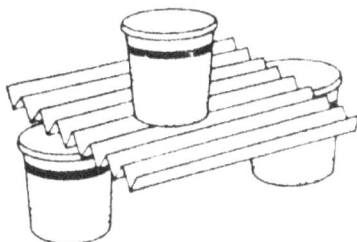

Ring Up

Hold up a pencil. Drop a finger ring over it. Say
the magic words, and the ring moves up and
down the pencil.

The secret is to attach a black thread to the
pencil eraser and to a button on your shirt or
coat. Put the ring over the pencil and thread.
Move it away, slowly, and the ring rises. Toward
you, it lowers

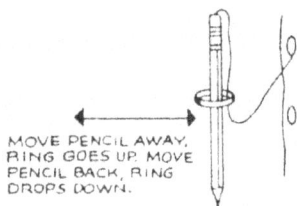

MOVE PENCIL AWAY,
RING GOES UP. MOVE
PENCIL BACK, RING
DROPS DOWN.

Magnetic Pen Cap

Take an ordinary pen with a cap on it and say
that the cap is magnetized, and won't leave the
pen. Every time you try to pull it off, it jumps
back on. Let a friend try . . . it won't work for
him, only you!

The secret is to hold the pen cap at the very tip.
When you pull it off so that the opening is at
the pen point, squeeze on the cap. It will jump
out of your hand, back onto the pen, and appear
as if it is magnetized. Practice!

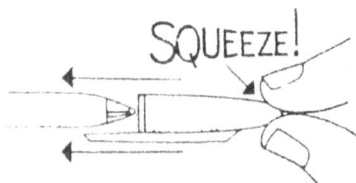

SQUEEZE!

Perplexing Pencil

An ordinary pencil will stick on your hand and will stay there until you tell it to drop.

The secret is to hold the pencil with your first finger, as in the picture. Note: You can also do this with a spoon, a comb, etc.

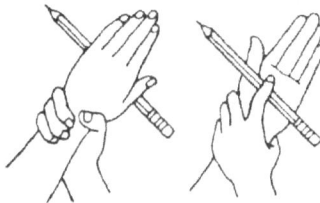

A Lotta Hot Air!

Put three small pieces of paper on the back of your hand. Now ask a friend to blow off two without disturbing the third. He can't do it but you can.

The secret is to hold down the third piece of paper with your finger.

MONEY
MIRACULOUS

What better prop could there be for magic than money? Everybody knows what money is . . . what it's for, what it looks like, what it feels like. And almost everybody uses money every day.

When you are a magician, people will always ask you to do a trick for them. When you can do a trick for them, even borrow the needed coin or bill from them to do it with, your reputation as a master magician will spread.

Coins are especially good for doing magic because they fit easily in your hand, and make clinking noises when dropped or rattled together.

For a colorful and interesting change, try using some foreign money for your tricks. Not only will people find them more interesting to look at, they'll know that only a real magician would use such exciting props!

Seeing Fingers

Borrow several coins and drop into a hat. Ask a person to mark one so it is different from the others. Then drop it into hat. Shake hat, hold high, reach in and pick the secret coin!

The secret is to put some wax under your fingernail before starting. Before you drop the secret coin into the hat, put the wax on the coin. Feel for the coin with wax in the hat.

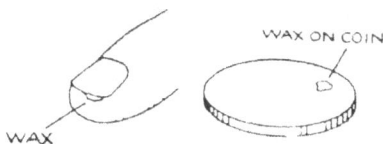

WAX ON COIN

WAX

Free Money

This is a great magical joke. Say "Now I'm going to do a really good trick. Can I borrow a dollar?" Take a dollar from someone, put it in your pocket and say, "Thank you . . . Now I'll do a good trick!"

The secret is presentation. Make them think you need the dollar to do a trick. When you put it in your pocket and say, "thank you," you make it look as if you are going to keep the dollar. A very funny joke!

Brave Balance

Place a strip of paper on the top of a glass and put a quarter on the edge of the glass on top of the paper. Tell everyone that the brave eagle on the quarter will now balance on the edge of the glass.

The secret is to hold the piece of paper as shown and give it a swift slap downwards. The paper will move away, but the quarter will balance. Practice!

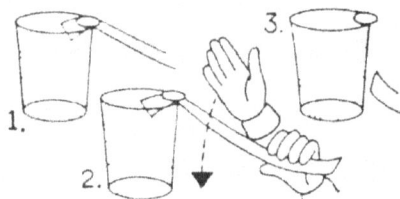

Dollar Power

Borrow a dollar bill (so people know it's not fake!) and break a pencil in half with it. Return the dollar and show the pencil is really broken.

The secret is to break the pencil beforehand and carefully put it back together again. When you "break" the pencil with the folded bill, put your finger alongside the bill. Your finger really does the work.

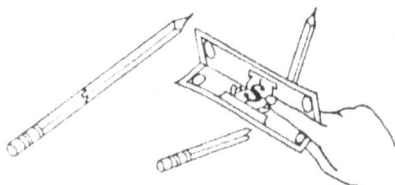

Growing Hole

Cut a small hole, about the size of a dime, in the center of a piece of paper. Now bet a friend that you can make a nickel or even a quarter pass through this small hole without ripping the paper!

The secret is to fold the paper in half and bend the edges inward. This stretches the hole so a coin can drop through, without ripping.
Study the picture.

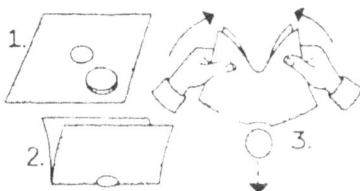

A Crafty Cup

Drink from a paper cup. Now drop a coin into it and shake it around to prove that it is there. Say the magic word, and the coin disappears. Show cup empty.

The secret is to cut a slot in the side of the cup at the bottom. The coin will slide out of it into your hand. Cover slot with finger to drink.

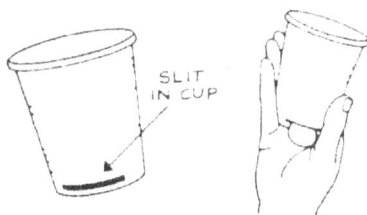

A Matchless Dime

Break a wooden match half way through and bend, but don't break entirely in half. Put it on a milk bottle (as in picture) and place a dime on top of it. Challenge a friend to make the dime drop into the bottle without touching the match or dime. He can't, you can!

The secret is to put a drop of water on the broken end of the match. The wood expands, and the dime falls in.

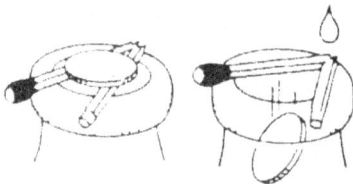

Vanished

You can vanish a coin by rubbing it between your palms. Start rubbing, and drop it "accidentally." Try a few more times, stop rubbing, and it has vanished.

The secret is to drop the coin "accidentally" and pick it up a few times. The last time, put the coin into your shoe when you pick it up. Pretend that it's still in your hand. (Practice to make this look magical).

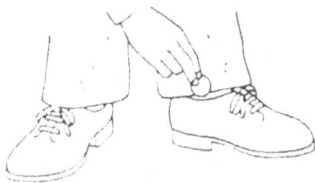

Up We Go

Put a dime heads up on a table. Challenge a friend to lift the dime with a straw. He can't, but you can!

The secret is to put a drop of water on the dime. Suck in on the straw and lift the dime.

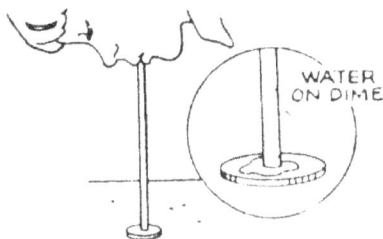

WATER ON DIME

Rising Coin

Drop a coin into a glass, say the magic words, and it rises up out of the glass.

The secret is to attach a piece of thin black thread to the coin with a piece of wax. Tie the other end of the thread to a button on your shirt or jacket. Slowly pull the glass away from you, and the coin rises.

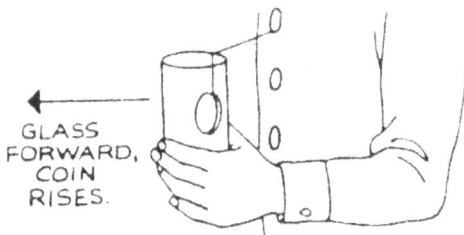

GLASS FORWARD, COIN RISES.

Amazing Escape

Have someone drop a coin into the drawer of an empty paper matchbox. Wrap box with a rubber band. Shake. The coin is inside. Wrap another rubber band. Shake. The coin has escaped.

The secret is to turn the box over when wrapping. Squeeze the sides, and the coin slides into your hand. Put the coin in your pocket when getting the rubber band.

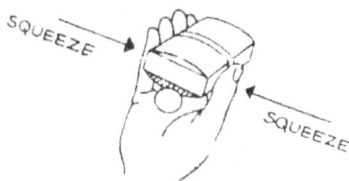

You'll Win Every Time

If you need to settle a bet, you can do it this sneaky way. Have some coins in your hand. Rattle them around, but don't show anyone. Ask if they are odd or even. No matter which they choose, you will win!

The secret is to use a dime, a nickel, and five pennies. If they say "even", you say "wrong, I have SEVEN coins." If they say "odd", you say "wrong, I have TWENTY cents." Only do this once, or they'll catch on.

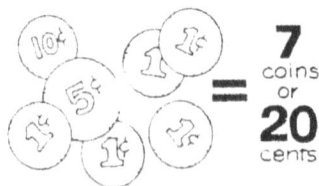

Enchanted Envelope

Show an ordinary envelope, and have someone drop a coin into it. Show the coin inside the envelope. Shake the envelope so they can hear it. Let them feel the coin inside the envelope. Suddenly tear it up and the coin has vanished!

The secret is to cut a small slit in the end of the envelope. Just before you tear it up, let the coin slide out of the envelope into your hand. After you rip it up, throw the pieces into the audience to be examined. Hide the coin after you do.

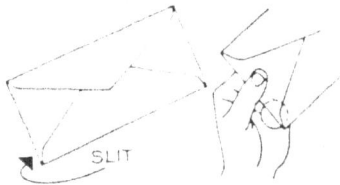

SLIT

Magic Money

Turn a paper cup upside down onto a piece of paper. Cup has no bottom. Person sees nothing when he looks into cup. Say magic words. Lift cup and find a coin inside.

The secret is to cut the bottom from the cup and paste a piece of paper (same color as other piece) over top of cup. As you turn cup over, slide coin underneath.

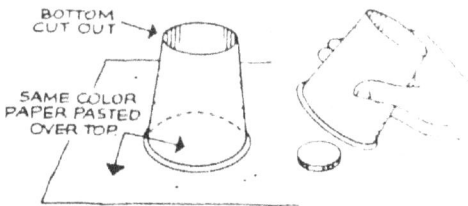

BOTTOM CUT OUT

SAME COLOR PAPER PASTED OVER TOP

Tube Magic

Drop a pencil through a cardboard mailing tube
to show that it is empty. Stand tube up on a
plate. Drop the coin inside. They hear it hit the
plate, but lift the tube and it is gone.

The secret is to paste a piece of paper with a
hole slightly larger than a pencil into one end of
the tube. Drop pencil through tube. Turn over so
the paper side is down to drop coin. Sound comes
out, but not the coin.

It's On My Mind

Ask someone to think of a coin. Now hold your
hand to your forehead and say, "Your coin is on
my mind!" Guess a penny. If it's right, you say.
"I knew it was on my mind." If it's wrong, you
say. "I thought it was on my mind!" For either
answer, remove your hand and there is a penny
stuck to your forehead.

The secret is to have a penny in your palm.
Press onto your forehead as you are
"concentrating."

Coin Escape

You have a coin that was used by the Great
Houdini! It can escape from anything! Wrap it up
in a piece of paper, hand the paper to a friend,
and the coin has vanished!

The secret is to fold the paper as in the
drawings. When you are making the last folds,
the coin slides out of the paper into your hand.

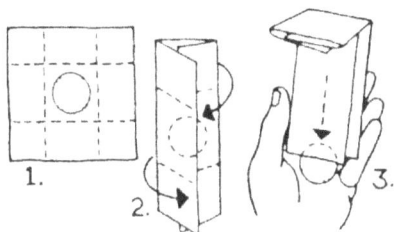

Cautious Coin

Borrow a coin from a friend. Put it on your
fingers and it balances. You can do it, but no one
else can.

The secret is to hold a pin between your fingers.
Lean the coin against the pin, and it balances.

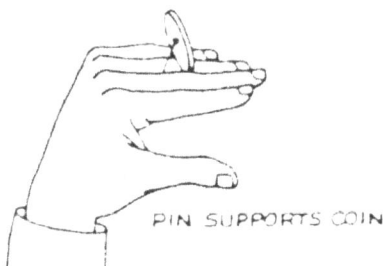

PIN SUPPORTS COIN

An Ear Full

Show both hands empty. Notice "something" behind your friend's ear. Reach behind his ear and pull out a coin.

The secret is to place a coin in your sleeve. Keep your arms bent up at the elbow so it won't fall out. After you show hands empty, drop arm and catch coin in your hand. Don't look down. Reach behind ear with penny already in hand.

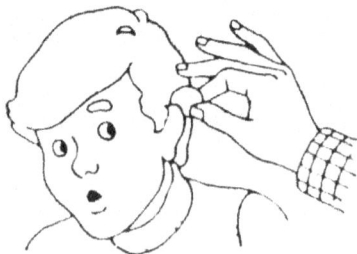

CRAFTY CARDS

C ards are the traditional favorite of magicians for astounding tricks. There are probably more magic tricks using cards than any other type.

P asteboards, as they were called in the old days, are extremely versatile. There are fifty two cards in a deck, each different. That means every time you ask someone to "pick a card" they have so many choices that they think you just couldn't be doing anything tricky. The magician also has fifty two different cards to make appear, disappear and change. Fifty four, if you count the two jokers . . . who usually look like Jesters. Cards also have four different suits (clubs, hearts, spades, and diamonds) in two colors (red and black), as well as number cards, picture cards and differently decorated and colored backs.

A skilled magician can do amazing things with cards, and so can beginners. And not every trick uses a whole deck. Many use just a few cards. Learn as many card tricks as you can, and then keep a deck with you to entertain whenever you want!

Balancing Cup

You can hold a playing card in your hand and balance a paper cup on top of it.

The secret is to use your first finger to balance as in the picture.

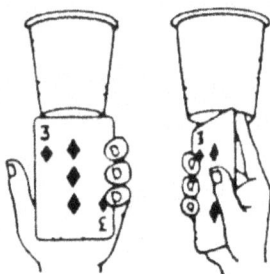

Crazy Cards

Put your hand flat on the table. Push a few cards under it one by one. Say the magic words, and slowly lift your hand. The cards rise with your hand.

The secret is to wear a ring, and put a toothpick under it. Push the first cards between toothpick and hand. These will hold the other cards.

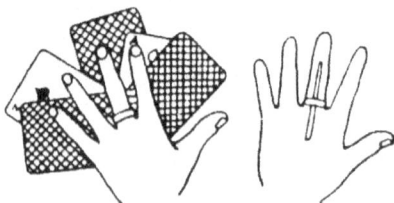

Magnetic Card

Have a friend pick a card out of the deck. After he looks at it, have him put it on top of the deck, and cut the cards. Spread all the cards face up on the table, and your finger is pulled to his card as if by a magnet!

The secret is to look at the card on the bottom of the deck. When he cuts the cards, that card is put right next to his card. His card will follow that card!

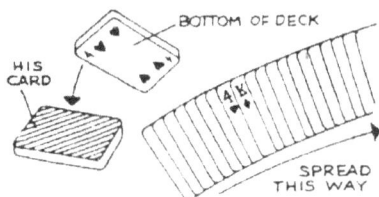

A Spooky Card

Someone picks a card out of the deck. You put the whole deck, along with the card, into the box. Then the card rises out of the deck.

The secret is to cut a long strip out of the card box, push up his card with your finger.
Note: Keep his card on top of the deck.

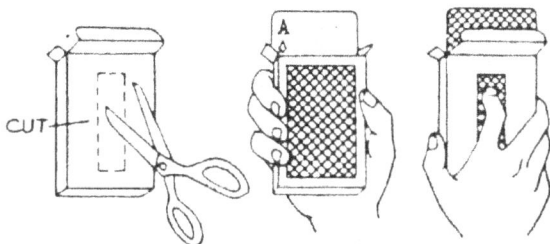

A Tricky Balance

Put a playing card onto the table, and balance a paper cup right on top of it.

The secret is in the card. Glue another card to the first card in the picture. Fold the card like a hinge. Don't let your audience see!

FRONT REAR

Sticky Cards

Have a friend take some cards out of a deck. Tell him to make them magically stick to the wall. He can't. You use the same cards and do it!

The secret of this trick is static electricity. Hold the card flat in your palm. Rub your feet against the carpet as you walk. Now slap the card quickly against the wall. It will stick.

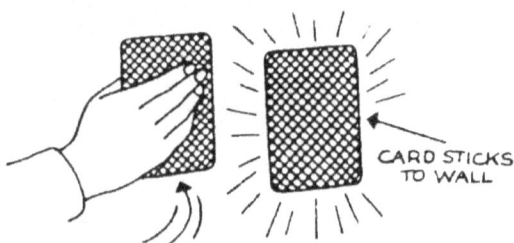

CARD STICKS
TO WALL

Passing Inspection

Take all four Jacks out of a deck of cards and put them in a line on the table. Ask a friend to inspect his troops. You know which two should be rejected, but he doesn't.

The secret is the "one-eyed Jacks". Can't go into battle with one eye!

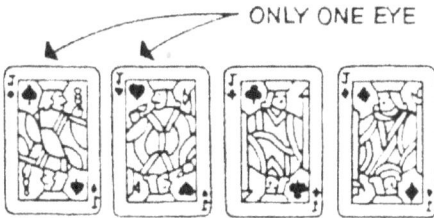

ONLY ONE EYE

Pick Me Prediction

Say that you have made a prediction of the card that a volunteer will select. Hand the volunteer a pack of playing cards. Tell him to look at each card, then call one out loud. You show your prediction . . . it matches!

The secret is the deck of cards that you hand the volunteer. Write on every few cards, "Please pick the 4 of Hearts," and "be a pal, please pick the 4 of Hearts", etc. Let it be your secret, don't tell the rest of the audience!

MYSTICAL MATCHES

M atches are good props for magic because they are so common, and there are so many things you can do with them. But some people don't
like to use matches, or your parents may not want you to, even if you never light them, so some of these tricks can be done with toothpicks instead.

M atches don't just light (which you should NEVER do unless you are supervised by an adult) but have many other useful properties. Some come in boxes, others in books. Some are wooden, and some are paper. The match heads come in a variety of colors, and they come in all different lengths.

A ll of these things make matches a very useful magical prop. And because everyone knows what matches are, it is unlikely that they'll think they are fake or somehow altered for your tricks.

All Shook Up

Show an empty matchbox. Say the magic words and shake it. There are loud noises, so something must be inside! Say the magic words again, and it is empty. Hand the box out for examination.

The secret is to use 2 boxes. Put some tacks or paper clips in one box, and fasten it to your arm with a rubber band. Pull your sleeve over it. When you shake the empty box using that hand, it makes the noise.

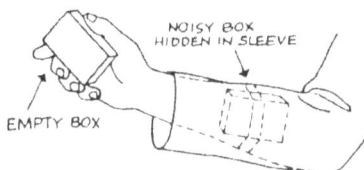

NOISY BOX
HIDDEN IN SLEEVE

EMPTY BOX

Marvelous Match Box

Place a matchbox on the back of your hand. Say "rise" and it stands up. Say "lie down" and it lies back down.

The secret is to partly open the drawer of the empty matchbox. When you put it upside down on your hand, close drawer, catching some skin between the box and cover (it won't hurt). Bend your fingers slowly, and the box will stand. Straighten, it will lie down.

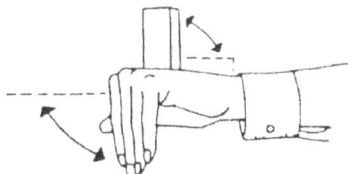

Mystical Matches

Put a bunch of matches or toothpicks on the table. Have a friend count them. He says there are eleven. You say you can turn the eleven into only nine, then prove it

The secret is to spell out the word "nine" using the matches, as in the picture.

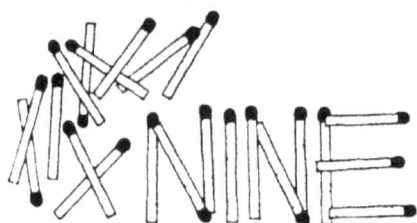

Edgy Match

Challenge your friend to make a match (taken out of a book of paper matches) land on its edge when dropped. He can't, but you can!

The secret is to bend the match in half. Drop it from about 2 feet, and it will land on its edge.

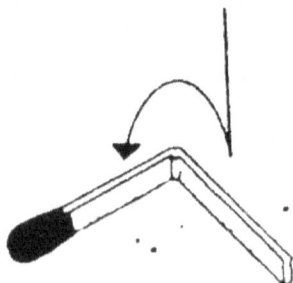

Steady Matches

Challenges a friend to balance a book of paper matches on its end. He can't do it, but you can!

The secret is to keep one or two matches outside the book cover when you close it. Bend these back (as in picture) and the book balances.

Amazing Match Box

Throw a match box up in the air. You predict if it will land label up or down.

The secret is to place a quarter between the bottom of the drawer and the box. The label will land up every time!

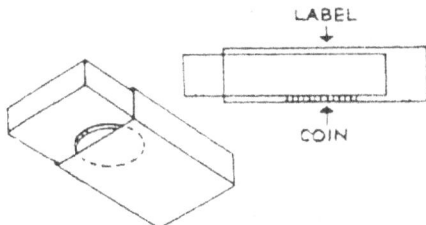

ITEMS COMMON

As you have probably noticed, you can do magic with just about anything. The more common and "normal" the item, the more amazing the magic seems. People expect magicians to use special boxes and props, but they are most impressed when the magic happens with things they see and use every day.

Oftentimes you will have the most fun doing magic with things that people don't expect you to do magic with. Cards are a common item, but everyone knows that magicians do card tricks. The same goes for money. The tricks you are about to learn use all kinds of different things that you can find around your house.

The more tricks you know, and the more common items that you can use to do them, the more you will be asked to do them and the better you will get! You will also be able to do magic any time, anywhere, using just what is at hand. This makes you an even more amazing magician!

Move Away

Challenge a friend to make a toothpick move away from an ordinary piece of soap. He can't, but you can!

The secret is to let the toothpick float in a bowl of water. Dip the soap into the water about an inch away from the toothpick. The toothpick will move away from the soap.

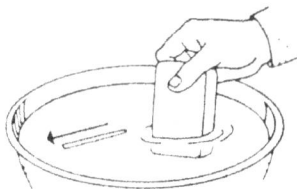

Hats Off

Put a glass of water on the table and put a hat over top of it. Tell your friends that you will drink the water without lifting the hat. Make slurping noises, and it's done!

The secret is to make them think that you drink the water. Then after they lift up the hat to look you grab the glass and drink the water. You drank the water, but you didn't touch the hat!

Growing Snake

You place a small bit of paper into water, and it grows into a long wiggly snake.

The secret is to slide the paper off a straw, squeezing it as small as it will get, but keep it lengthwise. (Don't crumple it into a ball.) When this is put into water, it looks as if a snake is growing before your eyes.

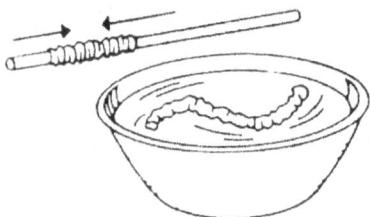

Dissolving Ball

Bounce a small ball on the bottom of a cup, proving the cup is solid. Rest the ball on the cup, hit the ball with your hand. It goes right through the cup.

The secret is to cut the bottom of the cup in a star shape, as in the picture. The ball will rest on the cup, until hit.

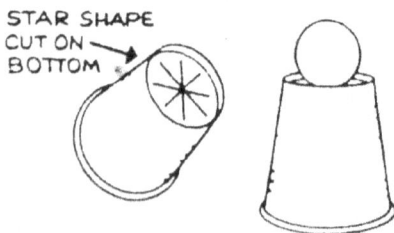

STAR SHAPE CUT ON BOTTOM

Back to Life

You open a box to show the finger of a long dead king. Command the finger to come back to life, and it magically begins to move. Put the top back on and put into your pocket.

The secret is to find a small gift box and cut a hole in the bottom. Put some cotton in the box, and stick your finger through the hole. Put some flour or baby powder on your finger to make it look "dead." When you put it away, just remove your finger.

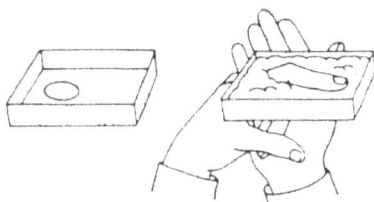

A Sticky Cigar

Hold your hand upright and place a cigar against it. Say the magic words, and it sticks there. Take it down and show there's no glue.

The secret is to put a pin in the cigar. Put the pin between your 2nd and 3rd fingers. When you pass the cigar around, pull it off the pin. Hide the pin while they look at the cigar.

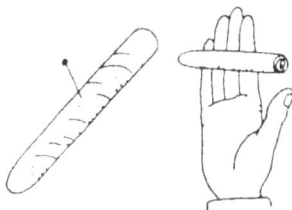

Restored String

Take a piece of string and make a loop in it. Cut it in half. Now bunch it up in your hand, get some "magic dust" out of your pocket, sprinkle it on, and the string is restored to one piece.

The secret is to make a fake loop out of string beforehand. Cut this loop instead of the string. Hide fake loop in pocket when getting "magic dust."

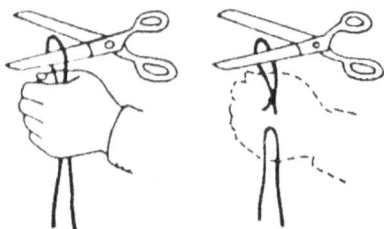

Surprising News

Take a piece of newspaper, show both sides to show it is normal. Now roll it into a tube, break it in half and find a handkerchief inside!

The secret is to paste the edges of two pieces of paper together on three sides, making a pocket out of the papers. Put a handkerchief flat inside and paste the last edge. It looks like one piece of paper.

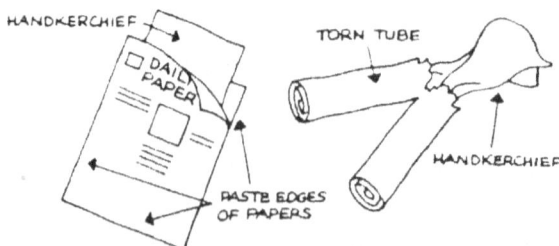

Crazy Cup

Place some paper clips into a paper cup and shake them around to prove that they are there. Rip cup to pieces. The clips have vanished.

The secret is to cut the cup as shown. Shake the clips on the half of the cup that is there. Let the clips fall into hand and hide as you rip cup. (Rip up into small pieces so no one notices the missing piece.)

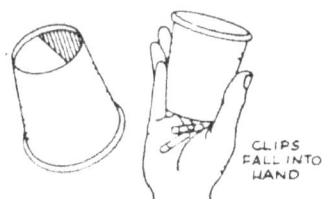

CLIPS FALL INTO HAND

Appearing Hanky

Show one hand empty. Show the other hand empty. Open first hand again and show that a hanky has appeared.

The secret is misdirection. Show one hand empty. While showing other hand empty, hold high in the air and look at it. As you are doing this, take hanky out of pocket with first hand. Now show it as if it magically appeared.

Shrinking Stack

Stack 6 or 7 checkers on a table. You can strike the stack with a ruler, and it won't fall, only the bottom checker moves.

The secret is to keep the ruler flat against the table. When you hit the bottom checker, it will move and the stack will shrink. You can do this until you have only one checker.

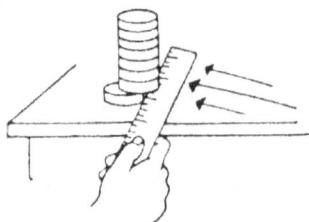

Brave Balloon

Blow up a balloon and say that it is a very brave balloon. Stick a few pins into balloon . . . it doesn't break. Now say that the balloon is scared of your friend. When he tries, it breaks.

The secret is, after blowing up the balloon, stick a few small pieces of clear tape in different places. Put the pins in the tape. When your friend tries, don't let him see the tape.

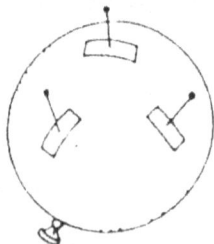

Crazy Cone

Show a small imitation ice cream cone, when you try to lick it, the ice cream vanishes. It reappears, and finally pops right out of the cone.

The secret is to make a cone out of cardboard or heavy paper. Cut a hole for your finger about one inch from the top. Use a small ball as ice cream. Keep hole towards you. Thumb controls ball.

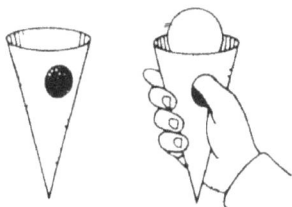

Topsy Turvy

Put three glasses on the table, two right-side up and one upside down as in the picture. Challenge a friend to turn them all upside down in only three moves, turning two at a time.

The secret is in the order that you turn them. The first time, turn over B and C. Second time A and C. Last time B and C. They're all upside down!

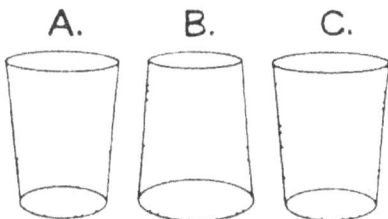

A.   B.   C.

Push Off

Put a hat on the table next to an upright piece of paper with a small hole in it. Now you will do the impossible, and push the big hat through the small hole. Make this sound very impossible.

The secret is to use a pencil and actually push the hat with the pencil through the hole, as in the picture.

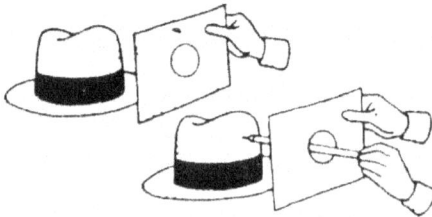

Swimming Needle

Challenge your friends to make a needle float in water. They can't, but you can!

The secret is to put a small piece of tissue on the water, and put the needle on the tissue, when the tissue sinks, the needle will float. Note: If the tissue doesn't sink, push it down with your finger.

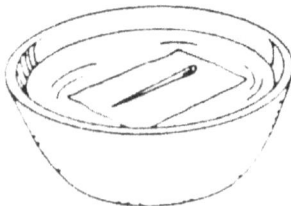

Knots Away

Challenge a friend to tie a knot in a handkerchief without letting go of either end of the handkerchief. It's impossible unless you know the secret.

The secret is to cross your arms as in the picture, and then pick up the handkerchief. By uncrossing your arms, you tie a knot in the handkerchief without letting go of the ends.

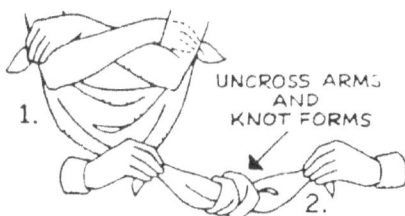

The Paper Rules!

Put a ruler on a table, hanging over about 4 inches. Now open up an ordinary newspaper and place it on top of the ruler. No matter how hard you hit the ruler, the paper won't lift off the table! Bet a friend that he can't do it. He'll think he can.

The secret is scientific. It works by itself. You may rip the paper or even break the ruler, but the paper will stay on the table.

Hole In One

You can make it look as if there is a hole in the middle of your hand, and show your friends how to do it too.

The secret is to roll a piece of ordinary paper into a tube. Look right through it with one eye, and put your other hand alongside it, as in the picture. Keep both eyes open, and it looks like a hole in your hand.

In Or Out

Place a soda bottle on its side, and put a cork in the opening, one that is a little too small for the bottle. When you ask a friend to blow the cork into the bottle, it will always pop out. He can't do it, but you can.

The secret is to use a straw, placed right in the center of the cork to blow the cork in.

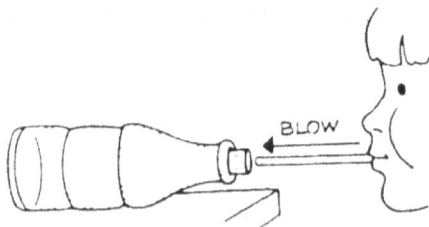

A Real Cut Up

Pu a piece of cardboard and through an envelope with its ends cut off. Cut it in half with scissors. Say the magic words, and the cardboard is whole, only the envelope is cut in half.

The secret is to make two slits in the back of the envelope and slip the cardboard through them as in the picture. This lets you cut the envelope without cutting the cardboard, by slipping the scissors between the envelope and cardboard.

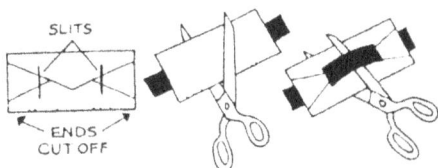

Can't Cut It

Place a piece of string on top of a sheet of paper. Fold the paper around the string and cut it in half. The paper is cut, but the string is unharmed.

The secret is to fold the paper into a flat tube, and cut around the string by pulling it out, as shown in the picture.

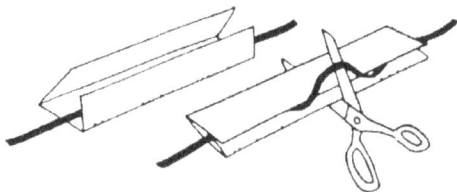

Can They Do It?

Redraw the figure below and see if a friend can draw it without removing his pencil from the page and without drawing over any lines. It can be done, but it's tough if you don't know how.

The secret is to draw it as in the second figure below.

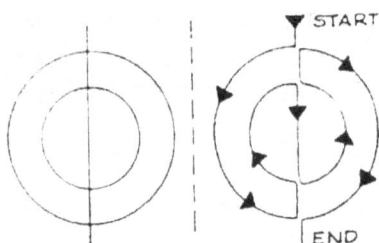

Over The Brim

Fill a glass full to the brim with water, and then add a little more by pouring it directly into the center of the glass, being careful not to get the edges wet. Now that it is almost overflowing, tell your audience that you can make the water rise above the brim without overflowing.

The secret is to drop pennies into the glass slowly. The water will rise above the brim!

Floating Arm

This is a funny trick that you can do with yourself or friends. Put your arm flat against a tree or wall and lean towards it, pushing as hard as you can (as if you are trying to push the wall). Now step away from the tree and your arm will rise into the air by itself! Creepy!

The secret is in your own reflexes. Your body does the work by itself. It works best if you push for at least 30 seconds.

Stick 'Em Up

Show butter knife, place it on your hand, and it sticks there.

The secret is to use a thin layer of rubber cement on your fingers and on the knife.

Clip Link

Take a dollar bill and fold it in three sections as shown. Now clip on two paper clips as shown, one to each end. Pull on the ends of the bill quickly, and the clips pop into the air, linked together.

The secret is in the placement of the clips. Do it as in the drawing, and it will always work by itself.

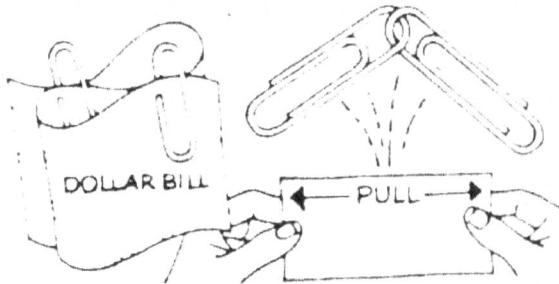

ILLUSIONS, PREDICTIONS & SPIRITS

I llusions are tricks of the eye. As the magician, you will know the secret behind these optical illusions, why they look the way they do, but even you will be fooled!

P redictions are a look in the future. When you make predictions and do other mental or mind-reading tricks, you are not only a magician, but a Mentalist as well!

F rom back in the times when magic was thought to be real, spirits have always played a part in making magic happen. Sometimes people, when they cannot explain something, make up an explanation of their own. Often, they chose to credit spirits (who were believed to be ghosts or souls of the dead) for making magic happen, both good and bad. But do spirits . . . good ones called sprites, or bad ones called demons, really exist? I don't know. Do you?

Tricky Illusion

Place down two pieces of colored paper. Ask someone which is larger. He picks one. Pick them up, say the magic words, and now the other one is larger.

The secret is an optical illusion. They are actually exactly the same size. Cut out two pieces of paper, different colors, in the same shape as the picture. Make them about two inches by four inches. One will always look larger.

Memory Magic

You hand a book to a person in the audience and tell him that you have memorized the entire thing. Go into the next room, have him call out a page number and announce the first line of that page.

The secret is to have a duplicate copy of the book in the next room. Performance hint: When you recite the line from the book, make it seem as though you are trying hard to remember it. You can even get a word or two wrong.

PAGE 137

Color Crazy

Your magic pencil will write any color someone chooses. Have someone name a color. If person says "blue," your pencil writes "blue."

The secret is to write the word for whatever color is named. A funny magic joke!

Tricky Fingers

Tear a strip of paper into three pieces. Hand to three people. Tell one to write a message. Leave the other two blank. Have them drop them all into a hat and hold it over your head. Reach in and pull out the only paper with a message.

The secret is to hand the piece of paper torn from the middle of the three to be written on. This has two rough edges. Feel for the two rough edges in the hat.

2 ROUGH EDGES

SECRET MESSAGE

Playful Prediction

Ask a friend to write a famous person's name on a piece of paper and put it in his pocket. You will read his mind and write it down. Now have him tell you the name. Say "I wrote 'that name'." Show him.

The secret is just to write the phrase "That Name" on the paper. Another magic joke!

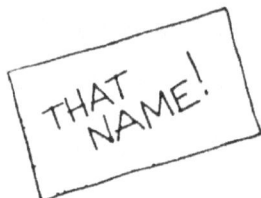

Mind Reading

You leave the room and have someone pick an item in the room. Now you return and ask him to concentrate. Your assistant asks, "Is it this?" You say "no." When he mentions the item, you say "yes." You can repeat it and always get it right.

The secret is that every time your assistant asks about an item that is a certain color that you have agreed upon (such as red), you know that the chosen item is going to be the next one!

Smart Spirits

Borrow a key. Ask audience to pick a person,
who hides key in his pocket . . . after you leave
the room. Return to room. Walk slowly through
audience. Concentrate. Spirits tell you the
person with key,

The secret is to secretly arrange for assistant to
sit like person with key (legs crossed, hand
under chin, etc.) Look for person sitting like
assistant.

Too Many Triangles

This is an optical illusion. Try to find all of the
triangles. How many are there? Better keep
counting, the real answer is 97!

The secret is to just remember that anything
with three sides and three corners is a triangle.
There are lots of small ones inside of bigger
ones. Good luck!

REMEMBER
THESE SHAPES!

The Spirits Know

You hold a string attached to a penny over
someone's hand. Ask the spirits. If she's a girl, it
will swing in a circle. A boy, in a straight line.
If they think you are making the penny move,
have them try. It will still work.

The secret is concentration. Don't try to swing
the penny. Just think hard . . . " Circle over
Girl" and "Straight Line over Boy." It will work
by itself. Have them do the same.

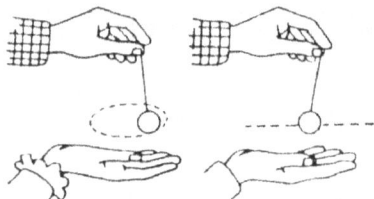

Spooky Seed

You drop a grape seed into a glass of ginger ale.
It sinks to the bottom. Now you command it to
rise by saying the magic words, and it does.

The secret is that the trick works all by itself!
The seed will sink because it is heavier than
water, but the bubbles in the ginger ale will
make it float up again.

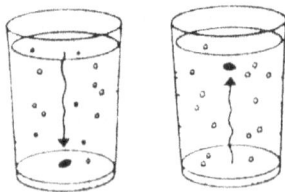

Touchy Triangles

Set eleven matches or toothpicks on a table to form five triangles as shown. Now ask a friend to remove three matches and be left with only two triangles. He won't figure it out.

The secret is to remove the three matches in the middle as shown. Now you have two triangles, one big and one small.

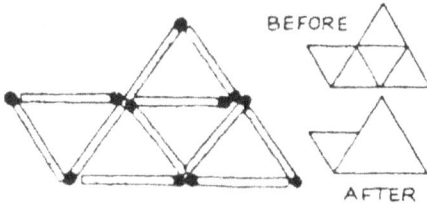

BEFORE

AFTER

Talking Chalk

Have someone hand you a piece of colored chalk behind your back. Concentrate. Give the chalk back, and name the color.

The secret is to rub some of the chalk on one of your fingernails. Look at the color secretly.

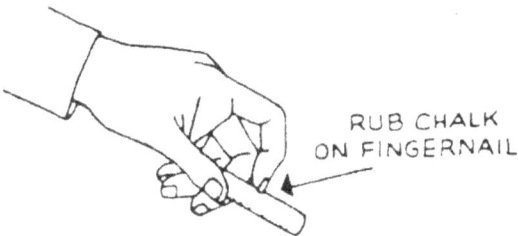

RUB CHALK ON FINGERNAIL

Spirit Writing

Hold a blank piece of paper over a toaster or
light bulb, say the magic words, and a message
appears.

The secret is to write a message on the paper
with lemon juice. When you put it over the hot
toaster, after a few moments what you wrote
will magically appear.

Have you done it?
Have you learned to be a **GREAT MAGICIAN**?

If so, you have earned your
Jester's Academy
Diploma!
Congratulations!

Dedication

This book is dedicated to Lori Karz, sometimes known as Enchantress Honeysuckle, for inspiring me to become the JestMaster. Who is more foolish, the Fool or the Fool who follows him?

(Yes, that is a snake she's holding!!)

Acknowledgements

Special Thanks to:
Lori Karz and Jane Keitel for data entry.
Marvin Kaye, for the great foreword.
Irv Koons for the whimsical illustrations.
All our wonderful Jesters who made **Ye Olde Cambridge Jester's Academy** such a hit at the New York Renaissance Faire for several years running.
And YOU, Fools and Jesters all!

About The Author

Jon Koons has written everything from genre fiction, to magic cereal packets, to scripts. His writings appear as books and audiobooks, as well as in anthologies, magazines, and periodicals. His children's picture book, *A Confused Hanukkah* is currently in development in Hollywood as an animated feature. Jon is Associate Editor for *Weird Tales Magazine*, as well as a regular contributor of short fiction and book reviews. Jon narrates and performs on numerous audiobooks, including his unique unabridged tour de force, *The Wonderful Wizard of Oz*. He heads up both Metamorphic Press and JestMaster Productions.

Dubbed "Renaissance Man" by the media, and oft known as "The JestMaster," Jon has appeared as an actor and singer On and Off Broadway, in Feature Films, on Television and in Commercials, and is a producing director of The Open Book Theatre Company in NYC. He is also a variety performer who does magic, juggling, ventriloquism, stilt-walking, fire-eating and a host of other cool stuff for events and parties. He's performed all over the world.

In his dubious spare time, Jon hangs out in New Jersey with his wife Mikki, a talented woodwind player and the love of his life; his miraculous son Merlin Ryan, a chip off the old block– heaven help him; their ferrets Groot and K9; and an ever changing cast of characters, both real and imaginary.

For more information about Jon's writing, jottings, scrawling, scribbles, books and audiobooks, go to *jonkoons.com*. For more info about all the other wild and wacky stuff he does, check out *jestmaster.com*.

Sign up for Jon's mailing list for news, contests and free stuff!
jonkoons.com

Jon Koons

Want even more Jon? Check out GOAT FILMS on YouTube for funny, funny films and videos! Please like and subscribe!

Look for this logo:

Metamorphic Press

We Only Print Good Stuff!

Irreverent Humor
(first time
in print
since 1976)

Irrelevent Humor
from award
winning author
Marvin Kaye

Humorous
SciFi
Yrl

Historical
Fiction

Classics

Stories for
Adults

Stories for
Kids

Insprirational
Pads and
Journals

More to come!
metamorphicpress.com

Write Down Your Patter and Performing Ideas!

Write Down Your Patter and Performing Ideas!

List The Tricks You Will Do In Order

List All The Stuff You Need To Put On Your Show

Figure Out What You Need For Your Costume

Write Down MORE Patter And Performing Ideas

Do you like to Draw and Doodle and Write
down all your most secret thoughts?

Of course you do!

Do you like Dragons?

You're a Magician now— of course you do!

Check out these great and mystical pads and
journals, each featuring a Fearsome (yet lovable)
Dragon and the Enchantress Honeysuckle.

Available from
Metamorphic Press
on Amazon!

www.ingramcontent.com/pod-product-compliance
Lightning Source LLC
Chambersburg PA
CBHW070534030426
42337CB00016B/2199